ISBN 1-59310-026-4

Cover image © PhotoDisc

Scripture quotations are taken from the King James Version of the Bible.

Published by Barbour Publishing, Inc., P.O. Box 719, Uhrichsville, Ohio 44683, www.barbourbooks.com

*Our mission is to publish and distribute inspirational products offering exceptional value and biblical encouragement to the masses.*

ecpa Member of the
Evangelical Christian
Publishers Association

Printed in the United States of America.
5 4 3 2 1

# 101 Things to be Thankful For

by Vickie Phelps

1. The love of family.

   *And I will bless them that bless thee, and curse him that curseth thee: and in thee shall all families of the earth be blessed.*
   GENESIS 12:3

2. True friends who are there regardless of circumstances.

   *A friend loveth at all times.*
   PROVERBS 17:17

3. God's Word, the bread of life.

   *It is written, That man shall not live by bread alone, but by every word of God.*
   LUKE 4:4

4. Freedom of worship.

*I will worship toward thy holy temple, and praise thy name.*
PSALM 138:2

5. Beautiful music to enjoy.

*Sing unto him a new song; play skilfully with a loud noise.*
PSALM 33:3

6. The warmth of a fire in winter.

*I will praise thee, O LORD, with my whole
heart; I will shew forth all thy marvellous
works.*
PSALM 9:1

7. Our forefathers who paved the way for us.

*Thus saith the LORD, Stand ye in the ways, and see, and ask for the old paths, where is the good way, and walk therein.*
JEREMIAH 6:16

8. A mother's love.

*For I was my father's son, tender and only beloved in the sight of my mother.*
PROVERBS 4:3

### 9. The singing of birds.

*The flowers appear on the earth; the time of the singing of birds is come, and the voice of the turtle is heard in our land.*

SONG OF SOLOMON 2:12

### 10. Rain in due season.

*Then I will give you rain in due season, and the land shall yield her increase, and the trees of the field shall yield their fruit.*

LEVITICUS 26:4

11. Two hands to perform tasks.

   *Whatsoever thy hand findeth to do, do it with thy might;*
   *for there is no work, nor device, nor knowledge, nor wisdom,*
   *in the grave, whither thou goest.*
   ECCLESIASTES 9:10

12. Laughter to express our joy.

   *Then was our mouth filled with laughter, and our*
   *tongue with singing: then said they among the heathen,*
   *The LORD hath done great things for them.*
   PSALM 126:2

### 13. The act of forgiveness.

*And be ye kind one to another, tenderhearted, forgiving
one another, even as God for Christ's sake hath forgiven you.*
EPHESIANS 4:32

### 14. Spring flowers.

*Thou waterest the ridges thereof abundantly: thou settlest the
furrows thereof: thou makest it soft with showers: thou blessest
the springing thereof.*
PSALM 65:10

### 15. Autumn leaf color.

*To every thing there is a season, and a time
to every purpose under the heaven.*
ECCLESIASTES 3:1

## 16. The instruction of a father.

*My son, hear the instruction of thy father, and forsake not the law of thy mother: for they shall be an ornament of grace unto thy head.*

PROVERBS 1:8–9

## 17. The innocence of children.

*But Jesus said, Suffer little children, and forbid them not, to come unto me: for of such is the kingdom of heaven.*

MATTHEW 19:14

## 18. Peaceful sleep.

*I will both lay me down in peace, and sleep: for thou, LORD, only makest me dwell in safety.*

PSALM 4:8

19. Tears expressing our joy or grief.

*They that sow in tears shall reap in joy.*
PSALM 126:5

20. A sister's love.

*Charity suffereth long, and is kind; charity envieth not; charity
vaunteth not itself, is not puffed up.*
1 CORINTHIANS 13:4

21. Sunshine after storms.

*The day is thine, the night also is thine:
thou hast prepared the light and the sun.*
PSALM 74:16

## 22. The ability to learn.

*A wise man will hear, and will increase learning; and a man of understanding shall attain unto wise counsels.*
PROVERBS 1:5

## 23. Kind words.

*A man hath joy by the answer of his mouth: and a word spoken in due season, how good is it!*
PROVERBS 15:23

## 24. The pursuit of happiness.

*Happy is he that hath the God of Jacob for his help, whose hope is in the LORD his God.*
PSALM 146:5

## 25. Lips that worship God.

*My soul shall be satisfied as with marrow and fatness;*
*and my mouth shall praise thee with joyful lips.*

PSALM 63:5

## 26. Eyes to enjoy the world around us.

*Truly the light is sweet, and a pleasant thing it is for the eyes*
*to behold the sun.*

ECCLESIASTES 11:7

## 27. The wisdom of our elders.

*Likewise, ye younger, submit yourselves*
*unto the elder. Yea, all of you be subject one*
*to another.*

1 PETER 5:5

### 28. Food on our table.

*And having food and raiment let us be therewith content.*
1 TIMOTHY 6:8

### 29. God-given talents.

*But now hath God set the members every one of them in the body, as it hath pleased him.*
1 CORINTHIANS 12:18

### 30. A place to worship God.

*I was glad when they said unto me, Let us go into the house of the LORD.*
PSALM 122:1

31. The warmth of sunshine.

*The day is thine, the night also is thine: thou hast prepared the light and the sun.*
PSALM 74:16

32. Fresh water to drink.

*And ye shall serve the LORD your God, and he shall bless thy bread, and thy water.*
EXODUS 23:25

33. Cool breezes on a hot day.

*He causeth his wind to blow, and the waters flow.*
PSALM 147:18

## 34. Laughter in the midst of sorrow.

*Even in laughter the heart is sorrowful.*
PROVERBS 14:13

## 35. Comfort from a good friend.

*Iron sharpeneth iron; so a man sharpeneth the countenance of his friend.*
PROVERBS 27:17

## 36. God's promises.

*The Lord is not slack concerning his promise, as some men count slackness; but is long-suffering to us-ward.*
2 PETER 3:9

37. The diversity of the four seasons.

*Thou hast set all the borders of the earth: thou hast made summer and winter.*
PSALM 74:17

38. A voice to sing songs.

*I will be glad and rejoice in thee: I will sing praise to thy name, O thou most High.*
PSALM 9:2

39. The breath of life.

*And the LORD God formed man of the dust of the ground, and breathed into his nostrils the breath of life; and man became a living soul.*
GENESIS 2:7

## 40. The love of a mate.

*Therefore shall a man leave his father and his mother, and shall cleave unto his wife: and they shall be one flesh.*
GENESIS 2:24

## 41. Children in the family.

*Lo, children are an heritage of the LORD: and the fruit of the womb is his reward.*
PSALM 127:3

## 42. Good health.

*Beloved, I wish above all things that thou mayest prosper and be in health, even as thy soul prospereth.*
3 JOHN 2

43. A godly heritage.

*When I call to remembrance the unfeigned faith that is in thee,*
*which dwelt first in thy grandmother Lois, and thy mother*
*Eunice; and I am persuaded that in thee also.*
2 TIMOTHY 1:5

44. Ears to hear.

*The ear that heareth the reproof of life abideth among the wise.*
PROVERBS 15:31

45. Coffee with a friend.

*He that is of a merry heart hath a*
*continual feast.*
PROVERBS 15:15

### 46. The confidence of a friend.

*A talebearer revealeth secrets: but he that is of a faithful spirit concealeth the matter.*

PROVERBS 11:13

### 47. Time spent with family.

*Blessed is every one that feareth the LORD; that walketh in his ways. Thy wife shall be as a fruitful vine by the sides of thine house: thy children like olive plants round about thy table.*

PSALM 128:1, 3

## 48. A godly mentor.

*Where no counsel is, the people fall: but in the multitude of counsellors there is safety.*
PROVERBS 11:14

## 49. Productive gardens.

*Build ye houses, and dwell in them; and plant gardens, and eat the fruit of them.*
JEREMIAH 29:5

## 50. Time spent conversing with God.

*I love them that love me; and those that seek me early shall find me.*
PROVERBS 8:17

51. Letters from a loved one.

*Heaviness in the heart of man maketh it stoop: but a good word maketh it glad.*
PROVERBS 12:25

52. A report of good news.

*As cold waters to a thirsty soul, so is good news from a far country.*
PROVERBS 25:25

53. Inspiring, caring teachers.

*Give instruction to a wise man, and he will be yet wiser: teach a just man, and he will increase in learning.*
PROVERBS 9:9

54. The desire for an abundant life.

*I am come that they might have life, and that they might have it more abundantly.*
JOHN 10:10

55. Hope for tomorrow.

*For thou art my hope, O Lord GOD: thou art my trust from my youth.*
PSALM 71:5

56. Good books to read.

*Whoso loveth instruction loveth knowledge.*
PROVERBS 12:1

57. The gift of God's grace.

*For by grace are ye saved through faith; and that not of yourselves: it is the gift of God.*
EPHESIANS 2:8

58. Courage to pursue our dreams.

*I can do all things through Christ which strengtheneth me.*
PHILIPPIANS 4:13

59. The comfort of a bed for sleeping.

*Stand in awe, and sin not: commune with your own heart upon your bed, and be still.*
PSALM 4:4

60. The beauty of the stars on a dark night.

*When I consider thy heavens, the work of thy fingers, the moon and the stars, which thou hast ordained; what is man, that thou art mindful of him?*
PSALM 8:3–4

61. The companionship of animals.

*And out of the ground the LORD God formed every beast of the field, and every fowl of the air; and brought them unto Adam to see what he would call them: and whatsoever Adam called every living creature, that was the name thereof.*
GENESIS 2:19

## 62. The harvest of a garden.

*For thou shalt eat the labour of thine hands: happy shalt thou be, and it shall be well with thee.*
PSALM 128:2

## 63. Modern technology.

*When the wise is instructed, he receiveth knowledge.*
PROVERBS 21:11

## 64. Rest after hard work.

*Six days thou shalt do thy work, and on the seventh day thou shalt rest.*
EXODUS 23:12

65. Prayer offered for you by a friend.

*Confess your faults one to another, and pray one for another, that ye may be healed. The effectual fervent prayer of a righteous man availeth much.*
JAMES 5:16

66. Beautiful artwork.

*I will call upon the LORD, who is worthy to be praised.*
PSALM 18:3

67. The skill of a good doctor.

*Many are the afflictions of the righteous: but the LORD delivereth him out of them all.*
PSALM 34:19

68. Rainbows after a storm.

*And it shall come to pass, when I bring a cloud over the earth, that the bow shall be seen in the cloud.*
GENESIS 9:14

69. Friends with strong shoulders to lean on.

*Ointment and perfume rejoice the heart: so doth the sweetness of a man's friend by hearty counsel.*
PROVERBS 27:9

70. Family holiday celebrations.

*Behold, how good and how pleasant it is for brethren
to dwell together in unity!*
PSALM 133:1

71. Air-conditioning in the summer.

*O give thanks unto the LORD; call upon his name: make
known his deeds among the people.*
PSALM 105:1

72. Mentors who care.

*The rich and poor meet together: the LORD
is the maker of them all.*
PROVERBS 22:2

### 73. An unexpected Valentine.

*Beloved, let us love one another: for love is of God; and every one that loveth is born of God, and knoweth God.*
1 JOHN 4:7

### 74. God's mercy.

*For the LORD is good; his mercy is everlasting; and his truth endureth to all generations.*
PSALM 100:5

### 75. Inner joy that makes you smile.

*Thou wilt shew me the path of life: in thy presence is fulness of joy; at thy right hand there are pleasures for evermore.*
PSALM 16:11

## 76. Employment.

*Whatsoever thy hand findeth to do, do it with thy might.*
ECCLESIASTES 9:10

## 77. The ability to laugh.

*A merry heart doeth good like a medicine.*
PROVERBS 17:22

## 78. The shade of a big tree.

*The shady trees cover him with their shadow; the willows of the brook compass him about.*
JOB 40:22

### 79. Victory after a battle.

*For whatsoever is born of God overcometh the world: and this is the victory that overcometh the world, even our faith.*
1 JOHN 5:4

### 80. Strength to run a race.

*For by thee I have run through a troop; and by my God have I leaped over a wall.*
PSALM 18:29

### 81. The small things in life.

*Bless the LORD, O my soul, and forget not all his benefits.*
PSALM 103:2

## 82. Spiritual direction.

*Blessed is the man that walketh not in the counsel of the ungodly, nor standeth in the way of sinners, nor sitteth in the seat of the scornful.*

PSALM 1:1

## 83. A field of wildflowers.

*The glory of the LORD shall endure for ever: the LORD shall rejoice in his works.*

PSALM 104:31

84. The majesty of mountains.

*As the mountains are round about Jerusalem, so the LORD is round about his people from henceforth even for ever.*
PSALM 125:2

85. The desire to smile.

*Happy is that people, whose God is the LORD.*
PSALM 144:15

86. Taking time to smell the roses.

*Be still, and know that I am God.*
PSALM 46:10

## 87. Opportunities to improve yourself.

*Hear, ye children, the instruction of a father, and attend to know understanding.*

PROVERBS 4:1

## 88. Communication with others.

*Righteous lips are the delight of kings; and they love him that speaketh right.*

PROVERBS 16:13

89. Common courtesy from others.

*Look not every man on his own things, but every man also on the things of others.*
PHILIPPIANS 2:4

90. Leisure time with friends.

*Be kindly affectioned one to another with brotherly love; in honour preferring one another.*
ROMANS 12:10

91. The ability to provide for your family.

*She looketh well to the ways of her household, and eateth not the bread of idleness.*
PROVERBS 31:27

### 92. Words of wisdom from a friend.

*Hear counsel, and receive instruction, that thou mayest be wise in thy latter end.*

PROVERBS 19:20

### 93. Another day.

*This is the day which the LORD hath made; we will rejoice and be glad in it.*

PSALM 118:24

### 94. Beautiful poetry.

*The Lord gave the word: great was the company of those that published it.*

PSALM 68:11

### 95. Courage when needed.

*Be strong and of a good courage, fear not, nor be afraid of them: for the LORD thy God, he it is that doth go with thee; he will not fail thee, nor forsake thee.*

DEUTERONOMY 31:6

### 96. Contentment.

*But godliness with contentment is great gain.*

1 TIMOTHY 6:6

97. A beautiful sunset.

*He appointed the moon for seasons: the sun knoweth his
going down.*
PSALM 104:19

98. A phone call from an old friend or relative.

*Pleasant words are as an honeycomb, sweet to the soul,
and health to the bones.*
PROVERBS 16:24

99. Early morning solitude with God.

*My meditation of him shall be sweet: I will
be glad in the LORD.*
PSALM 104:34

100. The power and beauty of a river.

*He sendeth the springs into the valleys, which run among the hills.*
PSALM 104:10

101. The privilege of doing good for others.

*Withhold not good from them to whom it is due, when it is in the power of thine hand to do it.*
PROVERBS 3:27